THE SIGNS ARE unmistakable: China is preparing to go to war.

For one thing, Xi Jinping can't stop talking about it, turning to the subject at every opportunity. At the annual meeting of the National People's Congress in March 2023, for instance, he repeated a favorite slogan: "Dare to fight."

Xi's message has quickly filtered down through the ranks. In the following month, the Eastern Theater Command of the People's Liberation Army, after completing provocative air and sea exercises around Taiwan, announced it was "ready to fight."

The Chinese regime is doing more than just talking, however. It is implementing the largest military buildup since the Second World War; it is trying to sanctions-proof itself; it is stockpiling grain; it is surveying America for nuclear weapons strikes; and, most ominously, it is mobilizing China's civilians for battle. China's military has, Cultural Revolution–style, launched a purge of officers opposed to war.

China's military is becoming powerful within the Chinese political system, Xi Jinping has domestic incentives to launch an attack, and Beijing can see there is little sense of urgency in Washington.

In one sense, the Communist Party of China has been at war with America for decades. The Party, despite official denials, has been engaged in "unrestricted warfare," a doctrine taken from the title of the infamous 1999 book by two Chinese air force colonels.

China's regime has been, among other things, using fentanyl to kill tens of thousands of Americans a year, stealing hundreds of billions of dollars of U.S. intellectual property annually, engaging in predatory trade practices for decades, and fomenting violence on American streets. Through Chinese-owned TikTok, the Party has been trying to divide the American public.

Now, however, there is also the prospect of "hot war" – "kinetic war," or war as Americans see it in the movies. General Mike Minihan, the commander of the Air Force's Air Mobility Command, said in a memo leaked on January 27, 2023, that he felt the U.S. would be in a war with China "in 2025." "The United States and China are on the brink of war and are beyond the ability to talk," wrote hedge fund superstar Ray Dalio the following April on LinkedIn, after a visit to Beijing.

There is now relentless momentum toward war. China's military is becoming powerful within the Chinese political system, Xi Jinping has domestic incentives to launch an attack, and Beijing can see there is little sense of urgency in Washington. All this translates into a further erosion of deterrence. America, in short, is not taking the threat of war as seriously as it must.

Perhaps the most disturbing trend in the world today is the militarization of the Chinese political system.

The People's Liberation Army, which reports to the Communist Party's Central Military Commission, steadily lost political power in the 1990s and during the first decade of this century. It is now, however, making a fast comeback.

The generals and admirals can thank Xi Jinping. In late 2012, he became the Party's general secretary – China's ruler – because, unlike his two immediate predecessors, he was acceptable to all the factions in the Communist Party. He was for just about everyone the least unacceptable choice because he was not identified with any of the factional groupings.

Once attaining the top spot, however, Xi decided that to rule effectively he needed a base, so he has looked to certain flag officers to be the core of his political support. As noted China-watcher Willy Lam put it at the time, Xi Jinping's faction was the military.

Specifically, Xi's faction is composed of military hardliners. He has relentlessly removed "corrupt" officers – in reality political purges of officers associated with his predecessors – and last decade reorganized the PLA from top to bottom. He is now in the process of eliminating officers who do not believe China should go to war, as the ongoing campaign against retired Air Force general Liu Yazhou suggests. Liu, who had argued against an invasion of Taiwan, has been handed a death sentence, which either has or will be commuted to life imprisonment.

Even though Xi now is thought to control the military, it may also be true that the military, the most cohesive faction in the Communist Party, is effectively telling Xi what to do or that Xi may feel he has to let the military do what it wants.

China's flag officers are evidently getting what they want. As they grab power, they are taking a bigger proportion of the country's resources. In 2022, the announced increase in the military budget was 7.1 percent while the economy grew 3.0 percent officially but in reality contracted. In 2023, Beijing announced it was increasing the military budget by 7.2 percent while the central government's gross domestic product growth target was only 5.0 percent.

This dangerous dynamic has been taking place for more than a decade. "China's military spending is growing so fast that it has overtaken strategy," said Huang Jing of Singapore's Lee Kwan Yew School of Public Policy in 2010. "The young officers are taking control of strategy, and it is like young officers in Japan in the 1930s. They are thinking what they can do, not what they should do."

In 1930s Japan, the country's military, like the Chinese military today, was emboldened by success and was ultranationalist. Then, like now, civilians controlled Asia's biggest army only loosely. Then, the Japanese media publicized the idea that Japan was being surrounded by hostile powers that wished to prevent its rise. And that is what the Chinese Communist Party is saying about China today.

China's hardliners, many of them in uniform, are setting the tone in Beijing. For instance, the People's Liberation Army in January and February 2023 surveilled U.S. nuclear weapons sites, including the Malmstrom, F.E. Warren, and Minot Air Force Bases, which house all of America's Minuteman III intercontinental ballistic missiles. The balloon also passed close by Whiteman Air Force Base, home to the nuclear-capable B-2 bomber fleet, and Offutt Air Force Base, the headquarters of Strategic Command, which controls U.S. nuclear weapons. China is obviously preparing a nuclear weapons strike on America and felt bold enough to violate American sovereign airspace to do that.

As the brazen balloon intrusion shows, China's flag officers are making their "military diplomacy" the diplomacy of the country. From admirals to ensigns and lieutenants to generals, China's officers have become dangerous, arrogant, and bellicose. By their own admission, they are spoiling for a fight. Full of bile, they are itching to use new weapons.

They will almost surely get the opportunity. The Chinese political system is now configured so that only hostile answers – and sometimes only the most hostile – are politically acceptable. Once, the Chinese tried to hide their aggressiveness. Now, they brag about it in public.

Chinese leaders, civilian and military, could be at their most dangerous. They are fueled by ambition, arrogance, and grievance, and they are not tempered by the horrors of war. In a speech on July 1, 2021, marking the centennial of China's ruling organization, Xi Jinping infamously said he would "crack skulls and spill blood." China's political system now has a bloodlust.

Xi last decade led the militarization of the political system. Now, he is mobilizing Chinese civilian society. The military is being given sweeping powers over civilian matters. Amendments to the National Defense Law, effective January 1, 2021, put the Party's Central Military Commission in charge of mobilization of civilians for war, taking away the responsibility from the central government's State Council, a civilian body.

The amendments, Richard Fisher of the International Assessment and Strategy Center said, "point to China's ambition to achieve 'whole nation' levels of military mobilization to fight wars and give the Central Military Commission formal power to control the future Chinese capabilities for global military intervention."

"The revised National Defense Law also embodies the concept that everyone should be involved in national defense," reports the

---

China's hardliners, many of them in uniform, are setting the tone in Beijing.

Communist Party's *Global Times*, summarizing the words of an unnamed Central Military Commission official. "All national organizations, armed forces, political parties, civil groups, enterprises, social organizations, and other organizations should support and take part in the development of national defense, fulfill national defense duties, and carry out national defense missions according to the law."

As Fisher, a Virginia-based China military analyst, noted, "For the past forty years, China's Communist Party has been preparing for brutal war, and now the ruling organization is accelerating its plans."

The acceleration is plain to see. China's Reservists Law went into effect March 1, 2023. Now, Beijing is establishing National Defense Mobilization Offices across the country. Moreover, China in the following month announced an enlargement of the pool of those subject to conscription in wartime to include veterans and college students.

Civilian mobilization is reaching into every

part of society. China's leader in March 2023 told private Chinese companies to "fight" alongside the ruling organization. The Communist Party by then was already implementing Xi Jinping's instructions. In the previous July, a Chinese entrepreneur making medical equipment for consumers said that local officials had demanded he convert his production lines in China to make items for the military. Communist Party cadres were issuing similar orders to other manufacturers, and the Party, he said, was operating once privately owned factories because their owners had fled, not wanting to stick around for Xi's war.

Chairman of the Joint Chiefs of Staff General Mark Milley in March 2023 told the House Armed Services Committee that war with China was not "inevitable." Nothing is inevitable, but Milley should ask himself one question: How many times in history has a militant regime embarked on a breakneck military buildup and not launched a war of aggression?

China's bold leader has personal reasons to use the military he is fast building. Xi Jinping's belligerent behavior is partly the result of how he changed Chinese politics by accumulating almost unprecedented power.

Xi inherited a political system in which leaders did not receive too much credit or too much blame because decisions were shared by all across the Politburo Standing Committee, the apex of power in China. In other words, power was parceled out across the Communist Party's factions, coalitions, and groupings. This system, therefore, eliminated the sharp and intense struggles that almost tore the country apart during the early years of the People's Republic. By the end of the first decade of this century, however, senior leaders began to believe that consensus governance was resulting in ineffectual leadership.

Enter new leader Xi Jinping. He ditched norms and understandings that kept peace in Beijing, and under the guise of a campaign against corruption he implemented what John Minnich of Stratfor called "the broadest and deepest effort to purge, reorganize, and rectify the Communist Party leadership since the death of Mao Zedong in 1976 and the rise of Deng Xiaoping two years later." Xi's motto, as stated by one of his political allies, is the Mao-era "You die, I live."

Xi grabbed supreme power, but with power he ended up with almost total accountability. At the same time, he jailed opponents, stripped them of assets, and punished their families. In the process, he raised the cost of losing political struggles. He must, therefore, believe he too is personally at risk.

Moreover, Xi is seeing a closing window of opportunity to achieve what he considers to be historic goals. In fact, the official Xinhua News Agency in 2020 ran a piece titled "Xi Stresses Racing Against Time to Reach Chinese Dream."

Xi is right. The regime at home is beset by simultaneous crises: continuing debt defaults, crumbling property prices, a stagnating economy, worsening food shortages, a deteriorating environment, and failing local governments. "China is at the edge of a cliff," says Peter Huessy of the Hudson Institute and GeoStrategic Analysis.

Moreover, China faces a long-term threat: the country's demographic collapse, the steepest projected decline in history. China, now with about 1.4 billion people, could lose somewhere from 900 million to a billion people this century. Although demographic disasters play out over decades, Xi faces a perception problem that is immediate. The world's understanding of the Chinese demographic crisis undermines China's image of strength, which Xi relies upon to intimidate others.

Pessimism now pervades China. The Chinese people think Xi has no answers and are fleeing. U.S. Customs and Border Protection reports that the number of Chinese refugees apprehended at the southern border during the first five months of FY 2023 was more than double the number for all of the previous year. Statistics from other jurisdictions show even larger percentage increases of Chinese seeking to enter the United States. "Sam," a Chinese migrant who entered America in January 2023 at Brownsville, Texas, put it this way to Axios: "It's like an animal stampede before an earthquake."

China is unstable, and Xi is now identified with failing domestic policies.

The Chinese who cannot leave their homeland are unhappy. Since late October 2022, there has been a series of extraordinary protests, some of them calling for the Communist Party and Xi to "step down." In short, the Chinese people are in a revolutionary mood these days. As the great China historian Yu Ying-shih said, the Communist Party has "lost people's hearts."

And the Party has lost hearts among the

privileged, not just the poor. Song Dandan, a famous actress with a well-connected family, in December 2022 took to a radio hotline to deliver an anti–Communist Party rant because her mother died after not being able to receive timely medical care because of Xi Jinping's "dynamic zero-COVID" rules. Her complaint went viral and showed that discontent across society was pervasive.

China is unstable, and Xi is now identified with failing domestic policies. He knows that, due to his changes to Party governance, he is being blamed for everything and can therefore lose everything. He may think his best solution to popular discontent is to start a war to rally the Chinese people. His Work Report to the Communist Party's Twentieth National Congress, a nearly two-hour speech, was notable for its dark view of the world and his threats to start conflicts.

Mao Zedong started the Cultural Revolution in 1966 to vanquish political enemies, by rallying the Chinese people to his side. He concentrated on changing China because he didn't have the means to go after other nations. Xi Jinping, also vulnerable domestically, has the means to attack foreigners to bolster support at home.

Xi now looks determined to go to war. His China is in crisis, and he is just about to make his crisis the world's crisis.

The Failure of Deterrence

War could come soon because the American political establishment is not expecting conflict and is certainly not prepared for it. General Milley in his March 2023 testimony said war with China is not "imminent." In the following month, Zack Cooper of the American Enterprise Institute told the Fox Business Network that "there's no reason to think we're on the brink of war right now."

The Pentagon thinks it has time to prepare. It hushed officers after the leak of the Minihan memo, which told his command to immediately prepare for war. Officially, senior officers talk about "the 2027 window," as Chief of

Naval Operations Admiral Mike Gilday put it in October 2022.

Currently, the U.S. Navy and U.S. Air Force do not seem overly concerned about war occurring in the short term. Both services have adopted "divest to invest" plans – in other words, the decommissioning of "platforms" to pay for the force of the 2030s and 2040s. For instance, the Navy is retiring mighty Ticonderoga-class cruisers and the Air Force wants to take F-22s, perhaps the world's most capable fighter, out of service.

The services are in a worsening budget-bind. The Biden administration defense budget for FY 2024, after taking into account probable inflation, proposes less money for the military. This shrinkage is occurring at a time of a large drawdown in weaponry and munitions due to the armament of Ukraine. A war game conducted by the House Select Committee on the Chinese Communist Party in April 2023 showed the U.S. would run out of antiship cruise missiles quickly, perhaps within a week.

A war game conducted by the House Select Committee on the Chinese Communist Party in April 2023 showed the U.S. would run out of antiship cruise missiles quickly, perhaps within a week.

"We are well within the window of maximum danger for the Chinese Communist Party invasion of Taiwan," said Representative Mike Gallagher, the Wisconsin Republican who chairs the committee. "Xi," said Representative Ashley Hinson, a committee member, "is running hypothetical invasion scenarios in his head every single day."

It's unlikely that President Joe Biden is planning defenses on a daily basis. He calls China a mere "competitor" and refuses to use "adversary" or "enemy." He is certainly not paying attention to the words of the Communist Party. In May 2019, *People's Daily*, the Party's self-described "mouthpiece" and therefore the most authoritative publication in China, carried a landmark piece declaring a "people's war" on America. This phrase has special meaning. "A people's war is a total war, and its strategy and tactics require the overall mobilization of political, economic, cultural, diplomatic, military, and other power resources, the integrated use of multiple forms of struggle and combat methods," declared a column carried in April 2023 by PLA Daily, an official news website of the People's Liberation Army.

The Party has not tried to hide its animosity toward America. On the contrary, it has gone out of its way to tell Washington how it feels. Most elements of America's political elite have chosen not to see the Chinese regime's antipathy toward America, and those who have noticed dismiss hostile words as mere rhetoric. Unfortunately, the hostility is significant.

The Party, with strident anti-Americanism, is establishing a justification to strike America. As James Lilley, Washington's ambassador to Beijing at the end of the 1980s and the beginning of the 1990s, memorably said, the Chinese always telegraph their punches.

They are now doing exactly that – just as America's deterrence of China is breaking down. The breakdown was especially evident in March 2021 when Yang Jiechi and Wang Yi, then Beijing's top two diplomats, met Secretary of State Antony Blinken and National Security Advisor Jake Sullivan in Anchorage. The pair of Chinese officials came to Alaska to rant and lecture America in public, not to engage in good-faith discussions. "So let me say here that, in front of the Chinese side, the United States does not have the qualification to say that it wants to speak to China from a position of strength," said Yang. The flight of the Chinese spy balloon in early 2023 proves that China's regime feels it can do whatever it wants.

Furthermore, Xi Jinping himself delivered an even more startling message in March 2023. "Change is coming that hasn't happened in 100 years," he said while bidding farewell to Vladimir Putin in Moscow at the end of their fortieth in-person meeting. "And we are driving this change together."

The Chinese leader was essentially saying that the international system was undergoing fundamental restructuring and that he was already the boss of the world. The U.S., he implicitly announced, could no longer stand in the way of his grand ambitions.

China's ambitious ruler has already transformed the international system by greenlighting Russia's invasion of Ukraine. On February 4, 2022, Putin and Xi met in Beijing for the opening ceremony of the Beijing Winter Olympics and issued a 5,300-word statement announcing their "no-limits" partnership. The statement was issued, not coincidentally, just twenty days before Russia attacked Ukraine. The invasion, by the way, occurred just four days after the end of the Beijing Games.

Since then, Xi Jinping has given Russia all-in support. The Chinese state, with elevated commodity purchases, effectively finances

Russia's war. Furthermore, China has been offering financial services to Russian banks cut off from SWIFT. Beijing is putting its diplomats in service of Russia. Chinese central government and Communist Party media outlets have been propagating ludicrous Russian narratives about the war. China, for instance, has been using Chinese-owned TikTok to amplify Russia's disinformation.

Moreover, China has been crossing Biden's red line by providing "lethal aid." Beijing fed location data, obtained from the Chinese-made drones that Ukraine had been operating, to the Russian military so that it could take out the Ukrainian operators. Chinese parties have also been selling drones and ammunition to Russia.

The Chinese leadership knows it has crossed America's red line, and, worse, it knows Biden knows it has done so. Consequently, Beijing must view Washington's periodic warnings as hollow and America as feeble. That translates into a further erosion of deterrence at a crucial moment.

> *Washington has, through indulgent and sometimes feeble-looking policies, imposed no costs. Chinese aggressors, predictably, watched closely and decided that there was no downside to engaging in provocative behavior.*

Unfortunately, American presidents, with the best of intentions, empowered the worst elements in Beijing by showing everybody else in the Chinese capital that aggression worked. How so? Washington has, through indulgent and sometimes feeble-looking policies, imposed no costs. Chinese aggressors, predictably, watched closely and decided that there was no downside to engaging in provocative behavior.

In fact, aggressive Chinese behavior has

resulted in the Biden administration backing down in crucial situations. "The State Department held back human rights-related sanctions, export controls, and other sensitive actions to try to limit damage to the U.S.-China relationship," Reuters reported in May 2023 after the January–February spy balloon incident. America, with misguided policies, is opening the door to war in Asia.

At the moment, the region is frantically working to close that door. Richard Fisher in mid-2022 pointed out that Chinese leaders liked "to elevate popular fears of conflict with China to undermine American alliances in the region." Beijing still does that, but now Chinese actions are forcing neighbors to work more closely to protect themselves.

China is the most powerful actor in the region, but it is not as powerful as the coalitions it is creating against itself. Australia, India, Japan, and the United States have formed the Quad and are operationalizing it with military cooperation. Australia, the U.K., and the United States joined together in the AUKUS pact in

2021. Japan and South Korea, putting aside a century of enmity, inked significant security arrangements during the spring of 2023. NATO is taking an interest in Asia and opening an office in Japan, and European nations are sending warships to patrol China's peripheral waters. If there is anything that can prevent Beijing from going on the attack in the next few years, it is Chinese leaders seeing their neighbors and others working to contain their aggressive plans. Nonetheless, deterrence is hanging by a thread.

TAIWAN

Xi Jinping could pick on many neighbors. He already has attacked south of the de facto border with India in various locations in the Himalayas, and he has been trying to dismember two archipelago nations, the Philippines and Japan. Most analysts assume, however, that Taiwan will be his main point of attack.

Xi has been clear that, one way or another, he will get Taiwan, mentioning it prominently in his speech on July 1, 2021, marking the centennial of the founding of China's ruling party. "Resolving the Taiwan question and realizing China's complete reunification is a historic mission and an unshakable commitment of the Communist Party of China," he proclaimed.

The Chinese certainly see not firmness in Washington but disarray, and this disarray is undoubtedly emboldening Xi Jinping to act even more aggressively.

Xi, with increasingly specific words, is establishing a deadline. "Looking further ahead, the issue of political disagreements that exist between the two sides must reach a final resolution, step by step, and these issues cannot be passed on from generation to generation," he said in October 2013. In March 2022, the Chinese central government, in its Work Report presented to the annual meeting of the National People's Congress, declared it was committed to "resolving the Taiwan question in the new era." This is the first time since Xi Jinping was named Communist Party general secretary in late 2012 that this once-a-year document included a time frame for annexing the island democracy.

Xi started using "new era" in November 2021 to signal that he will incorporate Taiwan into the People's Republic of China. Every anniversary that passes puts pressure on him to make good on his promise to take control of all "Chinese" territory.

Beijing, therefore, views most events in the context of Taiwan. When it comes to annexing its neighbor, the Chinese regime wants the world to think the United States cannot stand in its way. As Afghanistan was falling in August 2021, for instance, Beijing was portraying the U.S. as incapable. The semi-official *Global Times*, hours after the Taliban captured Kabul, asked how America could stand up to mighty China when it could not even deal with the ragtag Taliban.

The tabloid also pronounced this, referring to the U.S.: "It cannot win a war anymore."

Not surprisingly, as Afghanistan fell Chinese propaganda turned to Taiwan. In an editorial that August, the *Global Times* said that once a war breaks out in the Taiwan Strait, the island's defense will collapse in hours and the U.S. military will not come to help.

Will it? The United States for decades has managed the Taiwan situation by trying to placate Beijing. Washington has maintained a policy labeled "strategic ambiguity" – in other words, not telling either China or Taiwan what America would do in the case of imminent conflict.

Strategic ambiguity was developed in part to prevent Chiang Kai-shek from invading China, but after his passing and the democratization of the island a Taiwan-launched invasion has not been a real possibility. Nonetheless, Washington has kept the policy in place. Of course, strategic ambiguity has maintained the peace, but the policy has worked in a generally benign period. Unfortunately, China's threats show that the current era is anything but benign.

In reaction to changed circumstances, many in Washington are calling for "strategic clarity": definitively announcing that the United States will defend Taiwan from Chinese attack. President Biden on four occasions has clearly stated that the United States would fight to defend the island republic. White House and administration officials, both anonymously and on the record, contradicted the president all four times, however. The Chinese certainly see not firmness in Washington but disarray, and this disarray is undoubtedly emboldening Xi Jinping to act even more aggressively.

Nonetheless, there are two significant factors impeding an invasion. First, the primary objective of Communist China's foreign policy is not taking Taiwan or any other "lost"

Chinese territory. The primary objective is maintenance of Communist Party rule, and there are doubts the Party would survive an invasion of the island.

An invasion would be bloody. Richard Fisher, the China military analyst, believes China could lose about 50,000 combatants even if it achieved complete surprise in mobilizing thousands of barges, ships, and planes and in preventing others from coming to the island's defense. "Should China fail to gain complete surprise and the United States and Japan successfully mount a counterattack that included sea-air combat and combat on

---

The Pentagon in a November 2022 report forecast that China would quadruple its warheads from about 400 then to 1,500 by 2035.

Taiwan, China could lose 100,000 troops," Fisher said.

The Party's *Global Times* claims that the Communist Party's "casualty-tolerance" is "China's decisive advantage in any fight with the U.S." and that its "whole-of-society commitment to core national security priorities is legendary." A recent incident, however, suggests this claim is not true.

On the night of June 15, 2020, China's military launched a surprise attack on Indian troops south of the Line of Actual Control in Ladakh, high in the Himalayas. New Delhi immediately announced that twenty of its soldiers had been killed, but Beijing said nothing about its casualties until February 19, 2021, when it reported four troops had died. India puts the Chinese killed at forty-five, and the Russian news agency TASS issued a release agreeing with India's reporting of Chinese deaths.

Why is the Chinese regime so casualty-averse? Although China's people, due to continuous propaganda, are in favor of annexing

Taiwan at some point, many do not attach great priority to that mission, especially as they focus on worsening domestic problems. There is a growing chorus arguing that Beijing should deal with problems at home before devoting resources abroad.

There is also the deeply held belief that "Chinese should not kill other Chinese." Taiwan's people for the most part do not self-identify as "Chinese" – recent surveys show fewer than 3 percent see themselves as "Chinese" only – but the people of the People's Republic view themselves and Taiwan's people as of the same blood.

Furthermore, the Chinese in China mostly understand why the Taiwanese do not at this time want to be ruled by the Communist Party's horrible system. Finally, it appears most parents in China are not enthusiastic about sending their only child into battle and perhaps ending forever their family bloodline.

The second factor impeding an invasion centers on Xi Jinping's willingness to cede control of the People's Liberation Army.

Assembling a force for a combined air-land-sea operation would require giving a general or admiral almost complete control of the armed forces, making that flag officer the most powerful person in China. Any ceding of power would be hard for Xi in a political organization that fears what Mao Zedong called "the gun."

The Party's civilians have been in constant struggle with flag officers during most of the history of the People's Republic, even though the Chinese military is not a state army and reports to the Party. Marshal Lin Biao, once designated Mao's successor, almost certainly attempted a coup in 1971, which led to Lin's mysterious death and an almost complete purge of the high command. The trauma of that event is still felt in senior Communist Party circles.

Xi, however, might be able to relinquish control over the PLA if he felt he had the absolute loyalty of flag officers. Therefore, the success of Xi's purge of elements supporting Liu Yazhou is of great importance. It is not clear that, at this moment, China's leader feels comfortable enough to put himself at the mercy of anyone wearing a uniform.

Ultimately, China's Communist Party, whether ruled by Xi Jinping or not, feels it has to annex Taiwan. The island, once controlled by the Leninist regime of Chiang Kai-shek's Kuomintang, has now evolved, without violent revolution, into a vibrant democracy. That evolution, a hopeful development as seen by the world's democracies, has substantially increased the risk of war.

China's regime identifies the island's democracy as an existential threat because it fatally undermines the Communist Party's core narrative: that the Chinese people are not ready to govern themselves and therefore need a dictatorial system. Taiwan is a vibrant and successful democracy, and its existence proves that claim, which underpins the Party's top-down rule, to be wrong. Although the Taiwanese people, as noted, do not see themselves as "Chinese," the Chinese Communist Party does. Therefore, the regime feels it must, one way or another, destroy the "Chinese" democracy that thrives just 110 miles from its shores.

The existence of Taiwan's democracy, therefore, makes war likely. And now that Beijing has an overwhelming military advantage, how do Taiwan and its friends deter China? The United States and countries in the region are fast rebuilding their conventional forces but will be playing catch-up for at least a half decade.

The U.S. and its allies and partners are outgunned, ship for ship, plane for plane, soldier for soldier. As the Center for Security Policy's Frank Gaffney argues, today America needs more than just conventional weapons to prevent an invasion. Gaffney, an assistant secretary of defense responsible for nuclear weapons policy in the Reagan administration, says the United States has to convince Chinese aggressors that they will be destroyed by a first nuclear strike if they attack Taiwan.

So should the United States declare Taiwan to be under its "nuclear umbrella"? Many

Xi Jinping is not, as analysts like to say, competing with other countries within the Westphalian international system. He is not even trying to adjust that system so that it is more to his liking. He is trying to overthrow it altogether.

in the arms-control community believe, as a general matter, that a first-use doctrine does not deter. Daryl Kimball of the Arms Control Association has argued that the risk of "an uncontrollable and potentially suicidal escalation" is so high that the threat of using nuclear weapons "lacks credibility."

Although Henry Sokolski of the Nonproliferation Policy Education Center correctly states that "we don't really know what precisely deters and what does not," there is evidence suggesting that nuke threats can prevent conventional attacks. After all, during the Cold War Soviet armor could have rolled clear across Western Europe to the Atlantic Ocean and English Channel but never did, and NATO threatened to obliterate the Soviet Union should it have attempted to do so. Odds are, the threats stopped the Soviets in their tracks. And if the West's nuclear weapons did not deter, why did Moscow work so hard to prevent NATO in the early 1980s from deploying America's Pershing II missiles in Europe?

America had better figure this one out fast, because everyone acknowledges that China is racing to build its nuclear arsenal. The Pentagon in a November 2022 report forecast that China would quadruple its warheads from about 400 then to 1,500 by 2035.

"For decades, they were quite comfortable with an arsenal of a few hundred nuclear weapons, which was fairly clearly a second-strike capability to act as a deterrent," Secretary of the Air Force Frank Kendall stated in testimony in March 2023, referring to China. "That expansion that they're undertaking puts us into a new world that we've never lived in before, where you have three powers – three great powers, essentially – with large arsenals of nuclear weapons."

It also suggests that China is thinking of first strikes with nukes, as Chinese officials, both in and out of uniform, have throughout this century threatened. As Kendall testified, "I don't think I've seen anything more disturbing in my career than the Chinese ongoing expansion of their nuclear force." In any event, Beijing will almost certainly threaten to incinerate any country coming to Taiwan's assistance.

Will it come to that? Many believe the heroic resistance of Ukraine's people has convinced Beijing to hold off an invasion of Taiwan. Russia's unexpected difficulties must have reminded Chinese aggressors that there is no certainty in war. Yet there are other lessons that Beijing has undoubtedly learned. Perhaps the most dangerous one is the failure of Western sanctions to cut off the flow of cash to Moscow. For various reasons, Putin has been able to evade these measures or create workarounds. Xi Jinping, unfortunately, may think he can do the same should he go after Taiwan.

Ukraine, therefore, is the place where Xi is picking up tips for how to wage war. The future of Taiwan, consequently, could be decided on battlefields on the other end of the Eurasian landmass. And should Xi invade Taiwan while the war in Ukraine continues, there will be conflicts at both ends of that landmass.

Together with the fast-spreading insurgencies and battles in North Africa, it's apparent the world is transitioning from a period of general calm to one of constant turbulence. A Taiwan invasion will mean the world is descending into global conflict.

War can start in many ways.

A Chinese J-16 fighter jet engaged in a "dangerous maneuver" close to an Australian Royal Air Force Poseidon P-8 reconnaissance aircraft in international airspace over the South China Sea on May 26, 2022. The reconnaissance plane, according to the Australian Department of Defense, was engaged in "routine maritime surveillance activity."

The Chinese high-performance aircraft, Australia said, "accelerated and cut across the nose of the P-8, settling in front of the P-8 at very close distance." Then, the Chinese fighter "released a bundle of chaff, which contains small pieces of aluminum, some of which were ingested into the engine of the P-8 aircraft." The Chinese aircraft also fired flares as it was releasing the chaff, metal-coated filament used to confuse radar. This appears to be the first time any military had used chaff and flares for this purpose.

Fortunately, the Australian plane, a modified Boeing 737, was able to return to base.

The "chaffing" of the Australian P-8 might have resulted in catastrophe. "Chaff clouds ingested into the P-8's two engines could have caused an inflight emergency and the deaths of the aircrew," James Fanell of the Geneva Centre for Security Policy said.

China's May 26 act was intentional and of the type likely to damage the P-8, which is in fact what happened. Its actions, therefore, constituted an act of war, as Fanell, also a former U.S. Navy captain who served as director of Intelligence and Information Operations at the U.S. Pacific Fleet, mentioned.

China has engaged in a series of troubling intercepts of aircraft in recent years. For instance, a Chinese naval vessel "illuminated" an Australian P-8 with a laser over the Arafura Sea, which separates Australia from New Guinea, in February 2022. Canberra called the action a "serious safety incident." "Acts like this have the potential to endanger lives," the Australian Defense Force correctly said in a statement.

Moreover, on multiple occasions the Chinese military has lasered aircraft in the South China Sea and East China Sea. In 2018, the PLA "lit up" a U.S. Air Force C-130 from China's only official offshore military base, in Djibouti. The action injured two pilots. Fortunately, they were eventually able to land.

Furthermore, Canada in June 2022 complained of "unprofessional" Chinese air maneuvers that put its crews at risk as they participated in surveillance flights monitoring China's violations of North Korea sanctions. China's intercepts, Ottawa said, were becoming more frequent.

These incidents evoke the collision on April 1, 2001, of a Chinese F-8 fighter jet and a propeller-driven U.S. Navy EP-3 over the South China Sea. The incident, caused by the Chinese jet clipping the wing of the slow-moving American reconnaissance craft, resulted in the death of the fighter pilot and the U.S. Navy plane making an emergency landing at a Chinese base on Hainan Island. In clear violations of American sovereignty, China's military stripped the American plane of its electronic equipment and held the crew of twenty-four for eleven days.

China is obviously determined to provoke incidents. Beijing apparently thinks it can manage them because the U.S. and its partners do not impose costs for increasingly provocative Chinese behavior.

Moreover, China has been trying to intimidate others in international waters. The U.S. has been issuing warnings to Beijing for provocations – near collisions – in the South China Sea, especially around Second Thomas Shoal, which is occupied by the Philippines.

At that contested feature, Manila in 1999 grounded the *Sierra Madre*, a World War II–era hospital ship, and left a handful of marines on board to bolster its territorial claim to the shoal. China, employing what it calls "cabbage" tactics, has continually surrounded the tiny Philippine garrison with its small craft.

In March 2014, China escalated the situation by turning back two of Manila's resupply vessels, cutting off the troops stationed on the rusting *Sierra Madre*. "For fifteen years we have conducted regular resupply missions and personnel rotation without interference from China," said Philippine Department of Foreign Affairs spokesman Raul Hernandez at the time.

China has no colorable claim to Second Thomas Shoal. An arbitral panel in The Hague handed down the landmark decision of *Philippines v. China* in July 2016, invalidating Beijing's infamous "nine-dash line" territorial claim to almost all of the South China Sea and ruling against China on almost all its positions. The tribunal, for instance, held that Second Thomas Shoal was within the Philippine exclusive economic zone and on the Philippine continental shelf and so there was no basis for any Chinese claim to this feature.

Since then, China has continued to pressure the *Sierra Madre* by using rough tactics to prevent resupply. After provocative Chinese actions there and at other South China Sea locations, Vice President Harris in November 2022 and the State Department in April 2023 publicly warned Beijing that the United States was prepared to honor its obligations contained in the 1951 U.S.-Philippine mutual defense treaty. In other words, the Biden administration said it was willing to use force to, among other things, prevent Chinese craft from stopping the resupply of the grounded hospital ship.

Many worry about war if one of these dangerous Chinese aerial or sea intercepts results in an "accident." As a practical matter, there is no such thing as "accidental contact" when it comes to China. There will be such contact if the Chinese military wants to provoke an incident, and there will be no accident if it doesn't.

In the event China wants a crisis, the now highly militarized political system in Beijing will prevent Chinese officials from acting constructively. American administrations have continually sought to establish channels of communication to be used in crises, but they are essentially useless. China will talk only when it wants to.

China's Grand Ambitions

Ultimately, China intends to rule more than just Taiwan, the Philippines, and its other neighbors.

Xi for decades has been working to impose the Chinese imperial-era system, in which emperors believed they not only had the Mandate of Heaven to rule *tianxia* or "all under Heaven" but also that they were compelled by Heaven to do so. As then–Foreign Minister Wang Yi wrote in *Study Times*, the Central Party School's influential newspaper, in September 2017, Xi Jinping's "thought on diplomacy" – a "thought" in Communist Party lingo is an important body of ideological work – "has made innovations on and transcended the traditional Western theories of international relations for the past 300 years."

Wang with his time reference was pointing

to the Treaty of Westphalia of 1648, which established the current system of sovereign states. His use of the word "transcended," consequently, hints that Xi wants a world without sovereign states – or at least no more of them than China.

But Xi is not content with ruling just this planet. Chinese officials are talking about the moon and Mars as sovereign Chinese territory. "The universe is an ocean, the moon is the Diaoyu Islands, Mars is Huangyan Island," said Ye Peijian, the head of China's lunar program, in 2017, referring to features in the East China and South China Seas to which Beijing claims sovereignty. "If we don't go there now even though we're capable of doing so, then we will be blamed by our descendants. If others go there, then they will take over, and you won't be able to go even if you want to."

Ye's choice of examples is revealing. He compared the moon to the Diaoyu Islands, for instance. The Diaoyus, in the East China Sea, have been claimed and are in fact administered by Japan, but China also claims the outcroppings. Periodically, Chinese vessels intrude into the territorial waters around the Senkakus, Tokyo's name for the small islands, as a means of pressuring Japan to surrender them. In essence, Ye Peijian was saying that China would exclude others from the moon and Mars – and presumably the rest of the solar system – if it were in a position to do so.

Beijing has been dropping other hints of its ultimate intent. It calls its Mars rover Zhurong, for example. In April 2021, China's officials said the device was named after the god of fire in Chinese mythology. China did not say that Zhurong is also the god of the South China Sea, which Beijing claims as territorial water, and the god of war.

China is, once again, ruled by an aggressor with revolutionary ambitions. Xi Jinping is not, as analysts like to say, competing with other countries within the Westphalian international system. He is not even trying to adjust that system so that it is more to his liking. He is trying to overthrow it altogether. Xi's outlook can be summed up this way: one solar system, one state, one ruler.

Xi Jinping now has both the ambitions and the means to end decades of general peace. And he is fast making preparations to do so, mobilizing all of Chinese society.

China is going to war.

First American edition published in 2023 by Encounter Books,
an activity of Encounter for Culture and Education, Inc.,
a nonprofit, tax-exempt corporation.
Encounter Books website address: www.encounterbooks.com

Manufactured in Canada and printed on
acid-free paper. The paper used in this publication meets
the minimum requirements of ANSI / NISO z39.48–1992
(R 1997) (*Permanence of Paper*).

FIRST AMERICAN EDITION

Library of Congress Cataloging-in-Publication Data
is available for this title under the
ISBN: 978-1-64177-371-3 and the LCCN: 2023025825